The Very First Easter

Requests for information should be addressed to:
Zonderkidz, *Grand Rapids, Michigan 49530*

Library of Congress Cataloging-in-Publication Data:
The very first Easter / illustrated by Kelly Pulley.
    p. cm. -- (Beginner's Bible)
  ISBN 978-0-310-71827-7 (softcover)
  1. Easter--Juvenile literature. 2. Jesus Christ--Crucifixion--Juvenile literature. 3.
Jesus Christ--Resurrection--Juvenile literature. 4. Bible stories, English--N.T. Gospels.
I. Pulley, Kelly.
  BV55.V47 2009
  232.9'7--dc22
                                                                          2008015117

Editor: Kristen Tuinstra
Cover & interior design: Sarah Molegraaf

Printed in the United States of America

11 12 /NGW/ 7 6 5

The Very First Easter

Illustrated by Kelly Pulley

The Life of Jesus
Matthew 8–15

Jesus did many amazing things when he was alive on earth. Jesus healed sick people and calmed dangerous storms.

Jesus fed thousands of people from just a little bit of food. He could do these things because he is God's Son.

The True King
Matthew 21:1–11; Mark 11:1–11;
Luke 19:29–40; John 12:12–19

Jesus and his disciples went to Jerusalem for the
Passover Feast. Jesus told two disciples to bring
him a donkey. He told them where to find it.

Jesus rode the donkey into Jerusalem.
A big crowd welcomed him.

People waved palm branches and put them on the
road in front of Jesus. They shouted, "Hosanna!
Hosanna! Blessed is the king of Israel!"

The leaders in Jerusalem did not like Jesus. They saw how many people were following him, and they were angry about it. They were jealous.

Washing the Disciples' Feet
John 13:3–30

Jesus and his disciples gathered together for a
special Passover meal. Jesus knew he would be
leaving them soon.

After supper, Jesus removed his outer clothing.
He wrapped a towel around his waist. He filled a
bowl with water. Then Jesus washed and dried the
disciples' feet, one by one.

Peter said to Jesus, "Lord, you should never wash my feet."
Jesus said, "As I have washed your feet, you must wash each other's feet." Jesus showed them how to love and serve each other by washing their feet.

Jesus told the disciples, "One of you will turn against me tonight."

"Who will turn against you?" John asked.

"The one I give this piece of bread to," Jesus said. He handed it to Judas and said, "Do what you must." Judas quickly left.

The Last Supper
Matthew 26:17–29; Mark 14:12–25;
Luke 22:7–20

Jesus picked up a loaf of bread and thanked God for it. Then he broke it into pieces. He gave the bread to his disciples to eat. Jesus said, "This bread is my body. Every time you do this, think of me."

In the same way, he took a cup of wine and
thanked God for it. He gave it to the disciples
to drink. "This is my blood. It is poured out to
forgive the sins of many."

"The time has come for me to go away. Where
I am going, you cannot go yet. I am going to
heaven to prepare a wonderful new home for you.
But I will return to you soon."

"At first, you will be very sad. But do not be frightened. Soon you will understand and you will be filled with joy."

Jesus Is Arrested and Crucified
Matthew 26–27; Mark 14–15;
Luke 22–23; John 18–19

Jesus went to his favorite garden to pray. The disciples went along. Jesus prayed, "Father, I don't want to suffer the pain of the cross, but your will is more important. I am ready to give my life."

The leaders sent some soldiers to take Jesus away, even though he didn't do anything wrong. Peter wanted to protect Jesus. But Jesus said, "No. I must allow this to happen." All the disciples ran away, and the soldiers arrested Jesus.

The soldiers took Jesus to the leaders. They said,
"You say that you are the Son of God. We do not
believe you."

The soldiers took charge of Jesus. They made him carry a big wooden cross. They made him carry it to a place called Golgotha. There they nailed Jesus to the cross.

Jesus died on the cross.

Everyone who loved Jesus was very sad. But they forgot something important. Jesus had said he would see them again!

Jesus Is Risen!

Matthew 28:1–10; Mark 16:1–20;
Luke 24:1–12; John 20:1–18

After Jesus died, some of his friends laid his body in a big tomb. They sealed it shut with a large round stone. Soldiers guarded the tomb.

Three days later, the earth shook. An angel of the Lord came down from heaven and pushed the stone away from the tomb.

Some women were walking to the tomb. When they saw the angel, he said, "Do not be afraid. Jesus is not here. He has risen!"

When the women saw Jesus, they fell to their
knees to worship him. Jesus smiled and said,
"Go tell the others that I will see them in Galilee."
The women ran to tell the disciples the news.

Jesus Returns
John 20:19–20; John 14:2–3;
Luke 24:36–53

The disciples had locked themselves in a small room because they were afraid the leaders would send soldiers to arrest them.

Suddenly, Jesus appeared to them! He said,
"Peace be with you." They thought he was a
ghost. But Jesus said, "Touch my hands and my
feet so that you will know it is really me." The
disciples cheered! They were happy to see Jesus
again.

Later, Jesus told his disciples, "I gave my life so that you could be with me in heaven. I am going there to prepare a wonderful new home for you. When I come back next time, I will take you with me."

Jesus went up to heaven in a cloud. Someday, he will come back to take the people who love him to heaven. Jesus loved people so much, he died for everybody's sins.

The bestselling Bible storybook of our time—over 5 million sold!

9780310709626

Look for even more great books from The Beginner's Bible®:

The Beginner's Bible for Toddlers® • 9780310714088
The Beginner's Bible®—Book of Devotions—My Time with God • 9780310714811
My Sing-Along Bible • 9780310717270
All Aboard with Noah! • 9780310717263
I Can Read: Adam and Eve In the Garden • 9780310715528
I Can Read: Daniel and the Lions • 9780310715511
I Can Read: David and the Giant • 9780310715504
I Can Read: Queen Esther Helps God's People • 9780310718154
I Can Read: Jesus and His Friends • 9780310714613
I Can Read: Jesus Saves the World • 9780310715535
I Can Read: Jonah and the Big Fish • 9780310714590
I Can Read: Noah and the Ark • 9780310714583

Available at your local bookstore!